Flax Attack:

Delicious Flax Seed Recipes for a Healthier Lifestyle

BY: Nancy Silverman

COPYRIGHT NOTICES

© 2019 Nancy Silverman All Rights Reserved

Subject to the agreement and permission of the author, this Book, in part or in whole, may not be reproduced in any format. This includes but is not limited to electronically, in print, scanning or photocopying.

The opinions, guidelines and suggestions written here are solely those of the Author and are for information purposes only. Every possible measure has been taken by the Author to ensure accuracy but let the Reader be advised that they assume all risk when following information. The Author does not assume any risk in the case of damages, personally or commercially, in the case of misinterpretation or misunderstanding while following any part of the Book.

‖‖‖‖‖‖‖‖‖‖‖‖‖‖‖‖‖‖‖‖‖‖‖‖‖‖‖‖‖‖‖‖

My Heartfelt Thanks and A Special Reward for Your Purchase!

https://nancy.gr8.com

My heartfelt thanks at purchasing my book and I hope you enjoy it! As a special bonus, you will now be eligible to receive books absolutely free on a weekly basis! Get started by entering your email address in the box above to subscribe. A notification will be emailed to you of my free promotions, no purchase necessary! With little effort, you will be eligible for free and discounted books daily. In addition to this amazing gift, a reminder will be sent 1-2 days before the offer expires to remind you not to miss out. Enter now to start enjoying this special offer!

Table of Contents

Chapter I: Easy and Quick: Flax Seed Smoothies 7

(1) Flax Seed Citrus Green Smoothie 8

(2) Tropical Matcha and Vanilla Smoothie 10

(3) Blueberry Flax Smoothie... 12

(4) Flax Seed Banana and Coffee Smoothie 14

(5) Anti-Inflammatory Smoothie....................................... 16

(6) Flax Almond Banana Smoothie 18

(7) Almond Butter and Blueberry Smoothie 20

(8) Strawberry and Banana Flax Seed Smoothie 22

Chapter II: Start the Day off Right: Flax Seed Breakfast Recipes
.... 24

(9) Flax Seed Waffles... 25

(10) Homemade Breakfast Granola 28

(11) Oatmeal and Flaxseed Pancakes................................. 31

(12) Fiber-Packed Breakfast Bowl 34

(13) Flax, Apple, and Carrot Breakfast Muffins 36

Chapter III: Healthy Doesn't Have to Mean Boring: Flax Seed Lunch and Dinner Recipes 40

(14) Spiced Flax Seed Chicken Bites 41

(15) Flax Seed Crusted Tenders 44

(16) Beef and Flax Seed Meatballs 48

(17) Flax Seed Tortillas 51

(18) Black Bean Quinoa and Flax Seed Burger 53

(19) Veggie and Quinoa Bowl 57

Chapter IV: I Love Some Nibbles: Flax Seed Snack and Dessert Recipes 60

(20) Pistachio and Cranberry Bites 61

(21) Energy Bites 64

(22) Protein Peanut Butter Cookies 66

(23) Flaxseed Sticks 69

(24) Banana Chia and Flax Seed Pudding 73

(25) Chocolate Avocado Cookies 76

Chapter V: The More You Know: How to Use Flax Seed in Every Day Life 79

    Egg Replacer 80

    Breadcrumb Addition 81

    Add to Granola and Granola Bars 82

    Sprinkle over Salads 83

    Add to Any Smoothie 84

    Add to Peanut Butter 85

    Considerations 86

About the Author 87

Author's Afterthoughts 89

Chapter I: Easy and Quick: Flax Seed Smoothies

(1) Flax Seed Citrus Green Smoothie

This green smoothie is packed to the brim with nutritious ingredients, such as fruits and spinach, and the ultimate super food, flax seed.

Portion Size: 1 large smoothie or 2 small to medium smoothies

Preparation Time: 3 to 5 minutes

Ingredient List:

- 2 clementines, peeled
- 2 cups baby spinach
- 1 ripe banana, peeled
- ½ cup frozen pineapple chunks
- 2 Tbsp. flax seed, whole
- ½ cup water

~~~~~~

Instructions:

1: Pour the water into a blender. Add the pineapple chunks, baby spinach, banana, clementines, and flax seed.

2: Blend the mixture until smoothie.

3: Pour the green smoothie into the desired glasses and enjoy immediately.

(2) Tropical Matcha and Vanilla Smoothie

This green smoothie features a slew of beneficial ingredients, such as matcha powder, flax seed, kale, pineapple and yogurt.

Portion Size: 1

Preparation Time: 5 minutes

Ingredient List:

- ½ cup pineapple chunks, frozen
- ½ cup baby kale leaves
- 1 Tbsp. flax seed, ground
- ½ tsp. matcha powder, also known as green tea powder
- ½ cup Greek yogurt, vanilla
- 3 ice cubes

Instructions:

1: Place all the ingredients into a blender. Blend the mixture until it is smooth and creamy.

2: Pour the smoothie into the desired glass and enjoy immediately.

(3) Blueberry Flax Smoothie

This delicious smoothie is filled with superfoods to help fill your belly in a healthier way.

Portion Size: 1

Preparation Time: 5 minutes

Ingredient List:

- 1 cup frozen blueberries
- 1 Tbsp. ground flax seed
- ¼ cup Greek yogurt, full-fat
- Handful baby spinach
- 1 cup coconut milk

Instructions:

1: Blend all the ingredients together in a blender until smooth. Transfer the smoothie into a glass and enjoy.

(4) Flax Seed Banana and Coffee Smoothie

This smoothie recipe not only gives you all the benefits that flax seeds and bananas provide, but it also provides coffee lovers with that flavor and caffeine that they desire.

Portion Size: 1

Preparation Time: 5 minutes

Ingredient List:

- 1 ripe banana, peeled
- ½ cup almond or soy milk
- 1 Tbsp. flax seed
- 1 Tbsp. honey
- 2 Tbsp. brewed coffee, cold
- 2 Tbsp. walnuts, chopped

Instructions:

1: Pour the milk, coffee, and honey into a blender. Add the peeled banana, flax seed, and walnuts.

2: Blender the mixture until smooth.

3: Pour the smoothie into a tall glass. Consume immediately and enjoy.

(5) Anti-Inflammatory Smoothie

This smoothie contains ingredients that have shown to help reduce inflammatory flare ups without the help of prescription pain medication.

Portion Size: 1 large smoothie or 2 small to medium smoothies

Preparation Time: 5 minutes

Ingredient List:

- 2 cups pineapple chunks, frozen
- 1-inch piece ginger
- ½ cup raspberries, frozen
- 1 tsp. turmeric
- 1 cup coconut water or distilled water
- 1 Tbsp. flax seed meal
- 1 cup pain Greek yogurt

IIIIIIIIIIIIIIIIIIIIIIIIIIIIIIIIIIIIIIIIIIIIIIIIIIIIIIII

Instructions:

1: Place all the ingredients into a blender. Blend the mixture until it is smooth and creamy.

2: Pour the smoothie into the desired glass or glasses (if dividing the smoothies between multiple people) and enjoy.

(6) Flax Almond Banana Smoothie

Made with healthy ingredients, this smoothie makes a wonderful meal replacement that takes only a few minutes to throw together.

Portion Size: 1

Preparation Time: 5 minutes

Ingredient List:

- 1 ripe frozen banana, peeled and diced
- 1/3 cup Greek yogurt, fat-free and plain
- 2/3 cup almond milk, unsweetened
- 1 Tbsp. flaxseed meal, ground
- 1 ½ Tbsp. almond butter, creamy
- 1 tsp. honey
- 2 drops almond extract

Instructions:

1: Place the frozen bananas, yogurt, almond milk, flaxseed, almond butter, almond extract, and honey into a blender.

2: Blend the ingredients until smooth. Transfer the smoothie to a glass and enjoy.

(7) Almond Butter and Blueberry Smoothie

This smoothie is beyond creamy! You'll be delighted at how tasty and nutritious this beverage truly is.

Portion Size: 1 large smoothie or 2 small to medium smoothies

Preparation Time: 5 minutes

Ingredient List:

- ½ cups blueberries, frozen
- 1 ½ cups ripe banana, frozen and cut into chunks
- 1 Tbsp. almond butter
- 1 Tbsp. flax seed meal
- ¾ cup almond milk, plain and unsweetened
- 1 Tbsp. chia seed

Instructions:

1: In a blender, blend the blueberries, banana, almond milk, flax seed meal, and chia seeds until smooth.

2: Pour the smoothie into the desired glass(es). Garnish with some extra chia seeds if desired. Enjoy the smoothie immediately.

Tip: You can add 1 to 2 Tbsp. of protein powder to give this smoothie an extra kick.

(8) Strawberry and Banana Flax Seed Smoothie

Strawberry and banana goes hand-and-hand like peanut butter and jelly. And this delicious flax seed smoothie takes that combination to make an easy and healthy meal replacement or snack.

Portion Size: 1

Preparation Time: 5 minutes

Ingredient List:

- ½ ripe banana, sliced
- ½ cup unsweetened strawberries, frozen
- 2 Tbsp. flaxseed, ground
- 1 ½ cups milk, light soy or skim

Instructions:

1: Place all four ingredients in a blender and blend until the mixture is smooth.

2: Pour the smoothie into a glass and enjoy.

Chapter II: Start the Day off Right: Flax Seed Breakfast Recipes

(9) Flax Seed Waffles

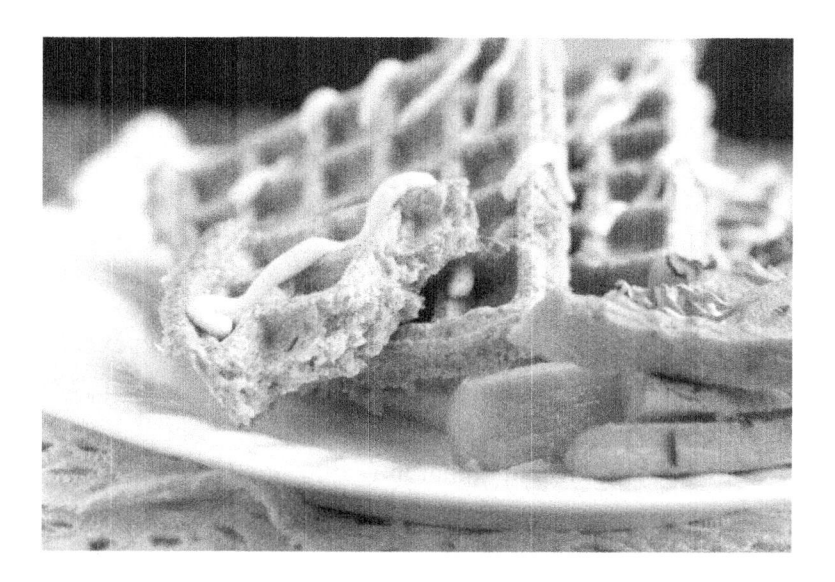

Gluten-free and low in carbs, this waffle recipe will fill you up for the day.

Portion Size: 4 to 6 waffles

Preparation Time: 15 to 20 minutes

Ingredient List:

- 2 cups flax seeds, ground
- ½ tsp. salt
- 3 tsp. baking powder
- 2 Tbsp. Stevia
- 1 ½ cups almond milk, unsweetened
- ¼ cup unsalted butter, melted
- 2 large eggs, room temperature
- 2 tsp. vanilla
- 1 ½ tsp. ground cinnamon

Instructions:

1: Preheat your waffle iron.

2: Place all the ingredients in a mixing bowl and stir until well combined. Let the bowl sit for several minutes. This will give the mixture a chance to thicken.

3: Cook the batter in the preheated waffle iron as you normally would. Continue cooking until you have used all the batter.

5: Serve the flax seed waffles while still warm with your favorite condiment, such as fruit, peanut butter, or syrup.

(10) Homemade Breakfast Granola

This breakfast granola can be stored for an extended period of time in an airtight container.

Portion Size: about 3 cups

Prep Time: 5 to 10 minutes

Bake Time: 18 to 20 minutes

Total Cooking Time: 23 to 30 minutes

Ingredient List:

- 3 cups rolled oats, old-fashioned
- ¼ cup flax seed
- 1 cup shelled pumpkin seeds
- ½ cup coconut flakes, unsweetened
- ¼ cup coconut oil
- ½ cup honey
- ½ tsp. salt

Instructions:

1: Preheat oven to 325-degrees. Line a baking sheet with parchment paper. Set to the side for the moment.

2: In a mixing bowl, stir together the coconut flakes, flax seeds, rolled oats, and pumpkin seeds until well combined. Set to the side for the moment.

3: In a separate bowl that is microwave-safe, combine the honey, salt, and coconut oil until well mixed. Heat in the microwave for 15 to 30 seconds.

4: Drizzle the honey mixture over the dry mixture and then toss to coat. Spread the mixture evenly onto the prepared baking sheet from 1.

5: Bake the granola in the preheated oven for 6 to 10 minutes. Stir the granola for several seconds before placing it back in the oven for an additional 6 to 10 minutes.

6: Remove the baking sheet from the oven and let the granola cool. Crumble the cooled granola into an airtight container until ready to use.

(11) Oatmeal and Flaxseed Pancakes

These cinnamon flavored pancakes contain oatmeal and flaxseed, which gives this breakfast staple a wonderful flavor and texture.

Portion Size: 4 pancakes

Preparation Time: 20 to 30 minutes

Ingredient List:

- 1/3 flour, whole-wheat
- 1 Tbsp. flaxseed
- 3 Tbsp. oats, quick-cooking
- ¼ tsp. cinnamon
- ½ tsp. baking powder
- 1/8 tsp. baking soda
- 1/16 tsp. salt
- ½ cup buttermilk
- 1 large egg, separated
- 1 Tbsp. canola oil
- 1 Tbsp. brown sugar, packed
- ½ tsp. vanilla

Instructions:

1: Mix the flour, oats, flaxseed, cinnamon, baking soda, salt, and baking powder together in a bowl. Set to the side for the moment.

2: In a second bowl, whisk together the egg yolk, brown sugar, vanilla, oil, and buttermilk. Gradually add this mixture into the dry mixture from 1. Mix until just combined.

3: Beat the egg white with a hand mixer until stiff peaks start to form. Gentle fold this into the mixture from 2.

4: Cook the pancake batter as you normally would, pour about ¼ cup of the batter onto a buttered or oiled hot griddle. When bubbles start to form on the batter, flip the pancake over and cook on the opposite side. Continue in this manner until you have used all the batter.

(12) Fiber-Packed Breakfast Bowl

This breakfast bowl is packed with fiber and gluten-free. It's a delicious way to give your body the energy it needs to start the day.

Portion Size: 1

Preparation Time: 5 to 8 minutes

Ingredient List:

- 1 Tbsp. flax seed, ground
- 2 Tbsp. chia seeds
- 2 Tbsp. hemp seeds
- 2 Tbsp. sunflower seeds
- ½ cup berries or apples, chopped
- 2 cups milk, almond

Instructions:

1: Mix the fruit, flax seeds, chia seeds, hemp seeds, and sunflower seeds together in a serving bowl.

2: When ready to eat, pour the milk over top and let sit for about 2 minutes.

3: Consume and enjoy!

(13) Flax, Apple, and Carrot Breakfast Muffins

These yummy breakfast muffins make a great grab-and-go meal for those busy mornings.

Portion Size: 6 to 12 muffins

Prep Time: 10 minutes

Bake Time: 10 to 15 minutes

Total Cooking Time: 20 to 25 minutes

Ingredient List:

- 1 ½ cups of whole wheat flour
- ¾ cup ground flax seed
- ½ cup packed brown sugar
- ¾ cup dry oats
- 1 tsp. baking powder
- 2 tsp. ground cinnamon
- 2 tsp. baking soda
- 2 cups apples, skinned and grated
- 2 cups carrots, skinned and grated
- 2 large eggs, room temperature
- ¾ cup of milk
- 1 cup dried cranberries
- 1 tsp. vanilla

Instructions:

1: Preheat oven to 350 F. Line a muffin tin with liners and set to the side for the moment.

2: Grind the oats to make oat flour by placing the oats in the blender and grinding the oats. Place the ground oats into a mixing bowl.

3: Add the grated apples and grated carrots into the mixing bowl with the oat flour. Stir in the flaxseed, whole wheat flour, packed brown sugar, baking powder, baking soda, and cinnamon until well combined. Set to the side for the moment.

4: In another mixing bowl, whisk the milk, vanilla, and eggs together.

5: Gradually stir the wet mixture into the dry mixture until well combined. Fold in the dried cranberries.

6: Divide the batter between the prepared muffin tin, filling each muffin opening about 2/3 full.

7: Bake the muffins in the preheated oven for about 10 minutes. Once the muffins are done, move from the oven and let cool.

Chapter III: Healthy Doesn't Have to Mean Boring: Flax Seed Lunch and Dinner Recipes

(14) Spiced Flax Seed Chicken Bites

Despite being easy-to-make, these chicken bites taste as though you spent hours in the kitchen when in fact it should take you less than 30 minutes.

Portion Size: 1

Prep Time: 8 to 10 minutes

Cook Time: 7 to 10 minutes

Total Cooking Time: 15 to 20 minutes

Ingredient List:

- 1 chicken breast, skinless and boneless
- ¼ cup flax seed, ground
- 1 tsp. ginger, ground
- 1 tsp. cumin
- 1 tsp. paprika
- 1/8 tsp. chili powder
- 2 ½ Tbsp. olive oil

Instructions:

1: Cut the chicken breast into small 1-inch bite-sized pieces. Set to the side for the moment.

2: In a mixing bowl, stir together the flax seed and the spices until well combined. Place the chicken pieces into the mixture and toss to coat thoroughly.

3: Heat the oil in a large skillet over medium heat. Add the coated chicken bites and cook until there is no pink on the inside, which should take about 3 minutes on each side.

4: Remove the chicken from the skillet and set on a serving platter. Serve while still warm.

(15) Flax Seed Crusted Tenders

These chicken tenders are coated in a crunchy flax seed coating and served with homemade sweet potato noodles.

Portion Size: 4

Prep Time: 10 to 15 minutes

Cook Time: 20 minutes

Total Cooking Time: 30 to 35 minutes

Coating Ingredient List:

- ¼ cup flaxseed
- ½ cup almond meal
- ¼ tsp. onion powder
- ½ tsp. garlic powder
- Pinch paprika
- Salt, to taste
- Ground black pepper, to taste

Ingredient List:

- 1 large egg, beaten
- 8 chicken tenders, boneless
- 1 Tbsp. olive oil
- 2 sweet potatoes, peeled
- Salt, to taste
- Ground black pepper, to taste
- ¼ tsp. chili powder

Instructions:

1: Preheat oven to 400-degrees. Line the bottom of a baking sheet with parchment paper. Set to the side for the moment.

2: Mix all the ingredients for the flax seed coating together in a shallow bowl. Set to the side.

3: In a second shallow bowl, add the beaten egg. Set to the side for the moment.

4: Dredge each chicken tender through the beaten egg, followed by the coating mixture, making sure that both sides of the chicken tender are well coated. Set the coated chicken tender on the prepared baking sheet from 1.

5: Bake the chicken tender in the preheated oven for about 15 minutes. The chicken should be cooked completely through with no pink inside.

6: While the chicken tenders are baking, heat the oil the skillet on the stove. Use a spiralizer cutter to cut the sweet potatoes into a noodle. Place the sweet potato noodles in the heated oil and season with the chili powder, salt, and pepper. Toss to coat and cook for about 7 minutes.

7: Serve the chicken tenders while still warm with a side of the sweet potato noodles.

(16) Beef and Flax Seed Meatballs

These Paleo-friendly meatballs are made using a grain-free breadcrumb substitution, which features flax seed.

Portion Size: 10 to 12 meatballs

Prep Time: 5 to 10 minutes

Bake Time: 12 to 14 minutes

Total Cooking Time: 17 to 24 minutes

Ingredient List:

- 2 Tbsp. flax seed, ground
- 2 Tbsp. almond flour
- 2 Tbsp. coconut flour
- ¼ cup mushrooms, finely chopped
- 1 pound ground beef, lean
- 1 large egg, lightly beaten
- 1 garlic clove, minced
- 2 Tbsp. onion, finely minced
- ½ tsp. salt
- ¼ tsp. ground black pepper

Instructions:

1: Preheat oven to 375-degrees.

2: In a small bowl, mix the flax seed, almond flour, coconut flour, and mushrooms together. Pour this mixture into a mixing bowl.

3: Add the beef, egg, onion, garlic, salt, and pepper into the mixing bowl from 2. Use your hands to knead the mixture until well incorporated.

4: Roll the mixture into balls that measure about 1 ½-inch in diameter. Set the meatballs on a baking sheet.

5: Bake the meatballs in the preheated oven for 6 to 7 minutes. Flip the meatballs over and bake for an additional 6 to 7 minutes.

6: Remove the meatballs from the baking sheet and set on a plate covered with paper towels. Let the excess grease drain from the meatballs.

7: Consume the meatballs as is or add to your favorite sauce.

(17) Flax Seed Tortillas

These easy to make tortillas are vegan-friendly and paleo compliant, and can be filled with the desired fillings, such as lunch meat or vegetables.

Portion Size: 2 tortillas

Preparation Time: 10 to 15 minutes

Ingredient List:

- ½ cup flax seed, ground
- 1/3 cup water
- Salt, to taste

Instructions:

1: Pour the water in a saucepan and set on the stove over medium heat. Bring to a boil. Add the ground flax seed and stir. Remove the saucepan immediately from heat.

2: Keep mixing the flax seed and water together until a dough forms. Separate the dough-like mixture into 2 parts.

3: Set a skillet on the stove over medium heat. And a bit of oil to coat the pan.

4: Place one of the separated dough balls into the heated skillet and, using a spatula, press the dough flat. Keep pressing until it is flattened to a tortilla-type shape. Flip it over and cook on the opposite side for a few minutes. Remove the tortilla from the skillet and set on a plate to cool.

5: Repeat 4 with the remaining portion of the dough.

6: Fill the tortillas with the desired fillings and enjoy.

(18) Black Bean Quinoa and Flax Seed Burger

These veggie burgers have a tender inside and a crunchy outside, with a spicy and smoky flavor.

Portion Size: 8 to 10 burgers

Prep Time: 30 to 35 minutes

Cook Time: 10 minutes

Total Cooking Time: 40 to 45 minutes

Ingredient List:

- 3 Tbsp. flax seed, ground
- 6 Tbsp. + 1 ½ cups water, divided
- 1 Tbsp. avocado oil
- 1 cup quinoa, uncooked
- 2 garlic cloves, peeled
- 30 ounces black beans, drained and rinsed
- ½ red onion, quartered
- 1 orange bell pepper, seeded and quartered
- 1 red chili pepper, seeded
- 4 cilantro stalks
- 1 Tbsp. liquid smoke
- 1 Tbsp. chili powder
- ½ tsp. cayenne pepper
- ½ tsp. cumin
- 2 tsp. sea salt
- Ground black pepper, to taste

Instructions:

1: Pour the 1 ½ cups of water and uncooked quinoa into a saucepan. Set the saucepan on the stove over high heat and bring to a boil. Reduce the heat to simmer, cover the saucepan, and let cook for 15 minutes. After the allotted time, remove the saucepan from heat. Keep the lid on the saucepan for an additional 5 minutes.

2: Process about three-fourths of the beans in a food processor. Transfer the processed beans into a mixing bowl. Add the remaining ¼ whole beans into the mixture. Set to the side for the moment.

3: Process the bell pepper in the food processor. You want the pepper to be chopped into tiny pieces. Transfer these pieces of pepper into the mixing bowl with the beans.

4: Pulse the garlic, chili pepper, cilantro, and onions in the food processor until finely chopped. Pour this mixture into the bowl from 3. Stir in the liquid smoke and all the spices until everything is well combined.

5: Mix the flax seed with 6 Tbsp. of water before mixing it into the mixture from 4.

6: Take ½ cup of the mixture and roll it into a ball before flattening it into a patty. Continue in this manner until you have turned all the mixture into a patty.

7: Cook the patties in an oiled skillet as you would a traditional beef hamburger. It should take about 4 to 5 minutes. Carefully flip the burger over and cook on the opposite side for an additional 4 to 5 minutes.

8: Serve the burgers on buns with the desired condiments, such as lettuce, tomatoes, ketchup, or pickles.

(19) Veggie and Quinoa Bowl

This quick and easy meal is filled with vegetables and flax seeds to give you a yummy and nutritious lunch or dinner.

Portion Size: 1 to 2

Preparation Time: 15 minutes

Ingredient List:

- Water
- 2 cups quinoa, uncooked
- 2 garlic cloves
- 2 Tbsp. nutritional yeast
- 2 Tbsp. flax seeds
- Sea salt, to taste
- Ground black pepper, to taste
- Greens and vegetables of your choice, such as peas, broccoli, shredded carrots, red onions, arugula, and yellow squash

Instructions:

1: Pour the 4 cups of water into a saucepan. Set on the stove over high heat. Stir in the quinoa and cover. Let the mixture boil for 10 to 15 minutes. Once the quinoa has absorbed the water, remove the saucepan from heat but keep it covered.

2: Heat the garlic, salt, and onion into a skillet. Set on the stove over medium heat. Pour ¼ cup of water into the skillet and cook until the vegetables are soft.

3: Add the remaining vegetables into the skillet and cook until soft. Taste the vegetables and adjust the spices as needed. You can also add any additional spices, such as basil, as desired.

4: Pour the cooked quinoa into a large mixing bowl. Add the flax seeds, nutritional yeast, and vegetables. Mix until well combined.

5: Transfer the mixture into a serving bowl and enjoy while still warm.

Chapter IV: I Love Some Nibbles: Flax Seed Snack and Dessert Recipes

(20) Pistachio and Cranberry Bites

No baking is required to make these healthy nibbles that are filled with energy-boosting ingredients.

Portion Size: 20 to 30 bites

Prep Time: 15 to 18 minutes

Chill Time: 30 minutes

Total Cooking Time: 45 to 48 minutes

Ingredient List:

- 1 cup dates, chopped
- ½ cup honey
- 1 Tbsp. flax seed, ground
- 1 Tbsp. chia seeds
- 1/8 tsp. salt
- 1 ½ cups dry oats, old-fashioned
- 1 cup cranberries, dried
- 1 cup pistachio nuts, shelled
- 1/3 cup white chocolate chips

Instructions:

1: In a food processor, add the dates, flax seed, chia seeds, honey, and salt. Pulse the mixture until smooth. Transfer the mixture into a mixing bowl.

2: Add the oats, cranberries, pistachios, and chocolate chips to the mixing bowl. Stir until all ingredients are well incorporated.

3: Cover the mixing bowl and let chill in the fridge for 30 minutes.

4: Shape the mixture into small 1-inch diameter balls. Store the energy bites in an airtight container for no more than 2 weeks.

(21) Energy Bites

These no-bake treats are a great way to satisfy that nagging sweet tooth without feeling guilty afterwards. What's even better is that these delicious little nibbles can help give you a boost of energy.

Portion Size: about 12 energy bites

Prep Time: 5 to 10 minutes

Chill Time: 15 to 30 minutes

Total Cooking Time: 25 to 40 minutes

Ingredient List:

- 1 cup oats, old-fashioned
- 2/3 cup peanut butter, creamy
- 2 Tbsp. honey
- ½ cup flax seeds, ground
- ½ cup chocolate chips, semi-sweet

Instructions:

1: Place all the ingredients into a mixing bowl. Using clean hands, mix the ingredients until well combined.

2: Put the mixing bowl in the fridge and let chill for 15 to 30 minutes.

3: Roll the mixture into bite-sized balls, the mixture should make 12 balls.

4: Store the energy bites in an airtight container in the fridge for no longer than 7 days.

(22) Protein Peanut Butter Cookies

These peanut butter cookies contain flax seed and are packed with protein.

Portion Size: about 18 cookies

Prep Time: 5 to 10 minutes

Bake Time: 10 to 15 minutes

Total Cooking Time: 15 to 25 minutes

Ingredient List:

- ¾ cup peanut butter
- ½ cup brown sugar, packed
- 1 large egg, room temperature
- 2 Tbsp. milk
- 2 tsp. vanilla
- 2 Tbsp. flax seed
- ½ cup + 1 Tbsp. protein powder, brown rice

Instructions:

1: Preheat oven to 350-degrees. Line a baking sheet with parchment paper. Set to the side for the moment.

2: Combine the peanut butter, egg, brown sugar, and vanilla together in a mixing bowl.

3: Mix in the vanilla and milk, followed by the flax seed and protein powder. Continue mixing until all ingredients are well combined.

4: Roll the cookie dough into balls that measure about a Tbsp. Set on the prepared baking sheet from 1. Flatten the balls and press a fork into each one to leave fork marks on them that you normally see on traditional peanut butter cookies.

5: Place the baking sheet in the preheated oven for 10 to 15 minutes. Remove the baking sheet from the oven and transfer the cookies to a wire rack. Let cool completely.

6: Store the cookies in an airtight container for up 4 days.

(23) Flaxseed Sticks

These delicious sticks are made with flax seed for a satisfying treat that won't throw off your healthy lifestyle.

Portion Size: about 36 sticks

Prep Time: 10 minutes

Bake Time: 20 minutes

Total Cooking Time: 30 minutes

Ingredient List:

- 1 ½ cups flour, all-purpose
- ½ cup flaxseed
- 1 tsp. salt, kosher
- ½ tsp. baking powder
- 2 tsp. onion powder
- ½ tsp. black pepper, ground coarsely
- 1 tsp. oregano
- 1 tsp. garlic powder
- 4 Tbsp. canola oil
- ½ cup milk, low-fat

Instructions:

1: Preheat oven to 375-degrees.

2: Mix the flour, flax seed, salt, pepper, baking powder, oregano, garlic powder, and onion powder until well combined. Set to the side for the moment.

3: In a second bowl, mix the oil and milk together. Gradually stir this mixture into the dry mixture from 2.

4: Place a piece of wax paper on a flat surface, such as your kitchen counter. Place the dough from 3 on the wax paper. Cover the dough with another wax paper the measures the same as the first.

5: Roll the dough out between the wax paper to a measurement of about 9x18-inches.

6: Cut the dough into strips that measure about 1/16 to 1/8-inch thick. Carefully twist each stick and set on a cookie sheet.

7: Place the sticks in the oven for 10 minutes. Carefully remove the cookie sheet from the oven and turn each stick over. Place them bake in the oven and bake for an additional 10 minutes.

8: Remove the cookie sheet from the oven and let cool on a cooling rack before storing in an airtight container for up to a week.

(24) Banana Chia and Flax Seed Pudding

Why purchase those pudding mixing in the baking aisle of your local grocery store when you can easily make your own healthier pudding that your family will love.

Portion Size: 1 to 2

Prep Time: 10 minutes

Chill Time: 2 hours

Total Cooking Time: 2 hours and 10 minutes

Ingredient List:

- 1 overly ripped banana, peeled
- 2 Tbsp. honey
- 2 ¼ cups almond milk
- ½ cup chia and flax seed blend

Instructions:

1: Place the peeled banana in a bowl and mash until smooth. Transfer the mashed banana into a small glass jar.

2: Pour the almond milk into the jar, followed by the honey. Secure the lid closed and shake the jar vigorously for several seconds.

3: Remove the lid from the jar and add the chia and flax seed blend. Secure the lid closed and vigorously shake the jar once again until well combined.

4: Place the jar in the fridge and let chill for about 2 hours, making sure to shake the jar occasionally during the chilling process.

5: Serve the pudding with your desired toppings, such as sliced bananas and chopped nuts.

(25) Chocolate Avocado Cookies

These vegan-friendly cookies are made with avocado, coffee and flax seed.

Portion Size: about 12 cookies

Prep Time: 10 minutes

Bake Time: 12 to 15 minutes

Total Cooking Time: 22 to 25 minutes

Ingredient List:

- 1 medium-sized avocado, skinned and pitted
- 1 Tbsp. ground flax seed
- ½ cup coconut sugar
- 3 Tbsp. water
- 3 Tbsp. chocolate chips
- ½ tsp. baking soda
- ½ cup cocoa powder, unsweetened
- Pinch ground cinnamon
- Pinch coffee granules, instant

Instructions:

1: Preheat oven to 350-degrees. Prepare a baking sheet by lining it with parchment paper. Set to the side for the moment.

2: In a small bowl, mix the water and the flax seed together. Set the bowl to the side and let the mixture start to thicken for about 3 to 5 minutes.

3: Combine the avocado, chocolate chips, sugar, instant coffee, ground cinnamon, and cocoa powder in a mixing bowl. Add the thickened flax seed mixture from 2 and mix until well incorporated.

4: Scoop the cookie dough onto the prepared baking sheet from 1. A cookie scoop works well to get the job done quickly and effectively.

5: Bake the cookies in the oven for 12 to 15 minutes. Once they are done, remove the cookies from the oven and transfer to a wire rack to cool. Store the cooled cookies in an airtight container.

Chapter V: The More You Know: How to Use Flax Seed in Every Day Life

Along with the recipes listed above, there are other methods you can use to incorporate flax seeds into your daily life. This chapter will discuss those methods so you get the most out of this useful ingredient in every way possible.

Egg Replacer

One thing that most people are unaware of is that flax seed, when mixed with water, can be used as an egg replacer in a lot of different recipes, such as in cookies, brownies, pancakes, and muffins. Merely mix 3 Tbsp. of warm water with 1 Tbsp. of milled flax seed. Allow the mixture to rest for about 10 minutes before adding it to the recipe.

Breadcrumb Addition

You can add 1 to 2 Tbsp. of flax seed for every cup of breadcrumbs. This gives the normally ho-hum breadcrumbs a boost of nutritional value. Another option is to forgo the breadcrumbs all together, when it is used as a binder such as in meatballs and meatloaves, and replace it with flax seeds.

Add to Granola and Granola Bars

Homemade granola and granola bars already have a lot of healthy ingredients, so adding in flax seed will only add to that nutritional value. A good general rule of thumb for adding this super food is to start with 2 Tbsp. of flax seed for every cup of oats in the recipe. You can alter this amount based on your needs, desires, and taste.

IIIIIIIIIIIIIIIIIIIIIIIIIIIIIIIIIIIIIIIIIIIIIIIIIIIIIIIIIIII

Sprinkle over Salads

Any salad can be made even healthier by sprinkling some flex seeds over top. The flax seed may look like ground black pepper when mixed in salads but you probably won't even taste it.

Add to Any Smoothie

While flax seeds in smoothies isn't a new thing, it is often overlooked, which is really a shame since it is one of the easiest ways to increase the amount of flax seed you are consuming. Typically, 1 to 2 Tbsp. of flax seed for 1 smoothie is the ideal amount. Keep in mind, however, that flax seeds absorb liquids, so you may have to add additional liquid to the recipe. The best thing to do is to play with the smoothie recipe and flax seed until you achieve the desired consistency.

Add to Peanut Butter

Enjoying a peanut butter and jelly sandwich for lunch or a snack? Sprinkle a bit of flax seed over top the peanut butter covered slice of bread before topping with the jelly-covered bread slice. You won't even taste the flax seeds but your body will thank you for the boosts of nutrients that it's getting.

Considerations

One of the great things about flax seed is that, in small amounts, you cannot even taste it. This allows you to incorporate it into most meals and dishes. Flax seed has a nutty flavor so keep that in mind when incorporating larger amounts into your recipes.

Like nuts, some people can be allergic to flax seed and this should be considered when making meals for other people. Furthermore, flax seed or any other ingredient for that matter, isn't a substitute for medical attention and you should never forgo your doctor's advice in favor of holistic or homeopathic remedies.

About the Author

Nancy Silverman is an accomplished chef from Essex, Vermont. Armed with her degree in Nutrition and Food Sciences from the University of Vermont, Nancy has excelled at creating e-books that contain healthy and delicious meals that anyone can make and everyone can enjoy. She improved her cooking skills at the New England Culinary Institute in Montpelier Vermont and she has been working at perfecting her culinary style since graduation. She claims that her life's work is always a work in progress and she only hopes to be an inspiration to aspiring chefs everywhere.

Her greatest joy is cooking in her modern kitchen with her family and creating inspiring and delicious meals. She often says that she has perfected her signature dishes based on her family's critique of each and every one.

Nancy has her own catering company and has also been fortunate enough to be head chef at some of Vermont's most exclusive restaurants. When a friend suggested she share some of her outstanding signature dishes, she decided to add cookbook author to her repertoire of personal achievements. Being a technological savvy woman, she felt the e-book realm would be a better fit and soon she had her first cookbook available online. As of today, Nancy has sold over 1,000 e-books and has shared her culinary experiences and brilliant recipes with people from all over the world! She plans on expanding into self-help books and dietary cookbooks, so stayed tuned!

Author's Afterthoughts

Thank you for making the decision to invest in one of my cookbooks! I cherish all my readers and hope you find joy in preparing these meals as I have.

There are so many books available and I am truly grateful that you decided to buy this one and follow it from beginning to end.

I love hearing from my readers on what they thought of this book and any value they received from reading it. As a personal favor, I would appreciate any feedback you can give in the form of a review on Amazon and please be honest! This kind of support will help others make an informed choice on and will help me tremendously in producing the best quality books possible.

My most heartfelt thanks,

Nancy Silverman

If you're interested in more of my books, be sure to follow my author page on Amazon (can be found on the link Bellow) or scan the QR-Code.

https://www.amazon.com/author/nancy-silverman

Printed in Great Britain
by Amazon